I dedicate this book to Harischandra Rajapaksha,
my grandfather, who loves nature just as much as I do.

Joe Rajapaksha

Illustrated by Iran C Perera

Hello! I am a bee.

I am sure you have seen me buzzing around.

I am that yellow insect with black stripes.

Insects are one of the most common types of invertebrates. Invertebrates do not have a backbone. Bees have six legs and at the end of each leg there are tiny little claws that are good for gripping onto stalks and flowers.

Bees also have three body parts: the head, the thorax, and the abdomen. There are two little things sticking out of a bee's head called antenna; these help bees to smell and feel things. They also help bees to talk to one another. Bees' bodies have lots of fuzzy hairs to keep them warm. Of course, they also have two wings which help them to fly.

Some bees are solitary. However, there are also some of us that are very social, so we stick together in a group called a colony and live together in a beehive. The beehive is made of beeswax.

We need to be very fast at flying because we are very busy doing lots of work. You may not know this, but we make something that lots of you eat daily.

It is something very...very...sweet. Can you guess? Honey!

Bees work very hard all day long to gather sweet nectar from beautiful flowers and sap from plants. But how do we make honey?

Well, we collect nectar using our long tongue called a proboscis, which slides into flowers and pulls out nectar. Our second stomach stores nectar, which is sometimes called the honey stomach, which does not digest it.

After collecting nectar, we return to the hive and transfer nectar to a younger worker bee waiting there. They chew it for about 30 minutes while adding enzymes to break down the nectar, which forms simple syrup.

Additionally, enzymes reduce the nectar's water content. The honey syrup is then deposited into hexagonal cells called honeycombs. The honeycombs are made from beeswax.

In our family, which is called a colony, we all have different jobs.

1. Queen Bee: Our mummy is the queen. She is the one who leads all her little bees which are called workers and drones.

2. Workers: They are all females. The workers look after the nest. Some workers look after the queen by cleaning and feeding her. Other workers are busy collecting nectar to make honey.

3. Drones: In a colony there are a few males with large eyes and they are called drones.

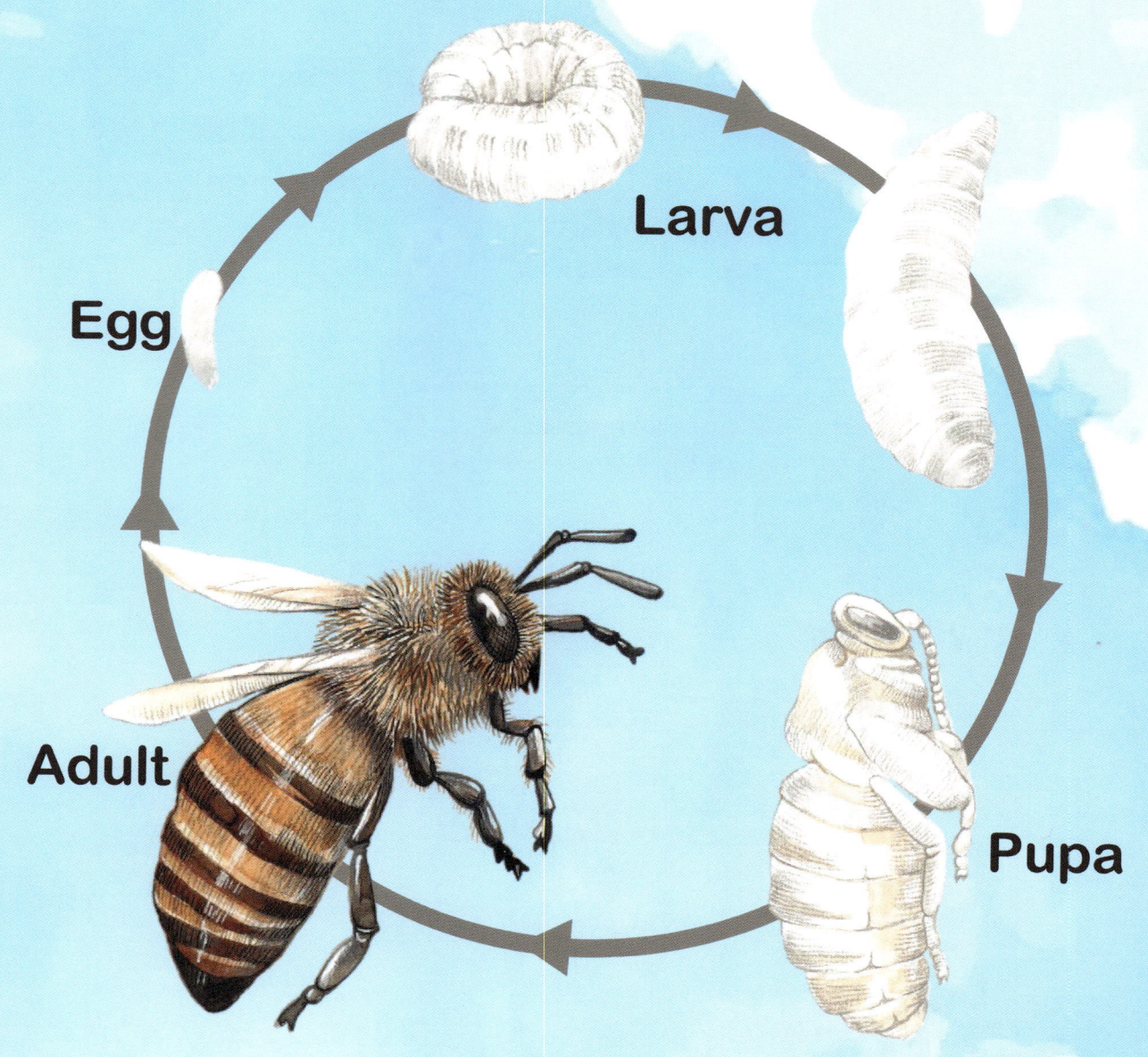

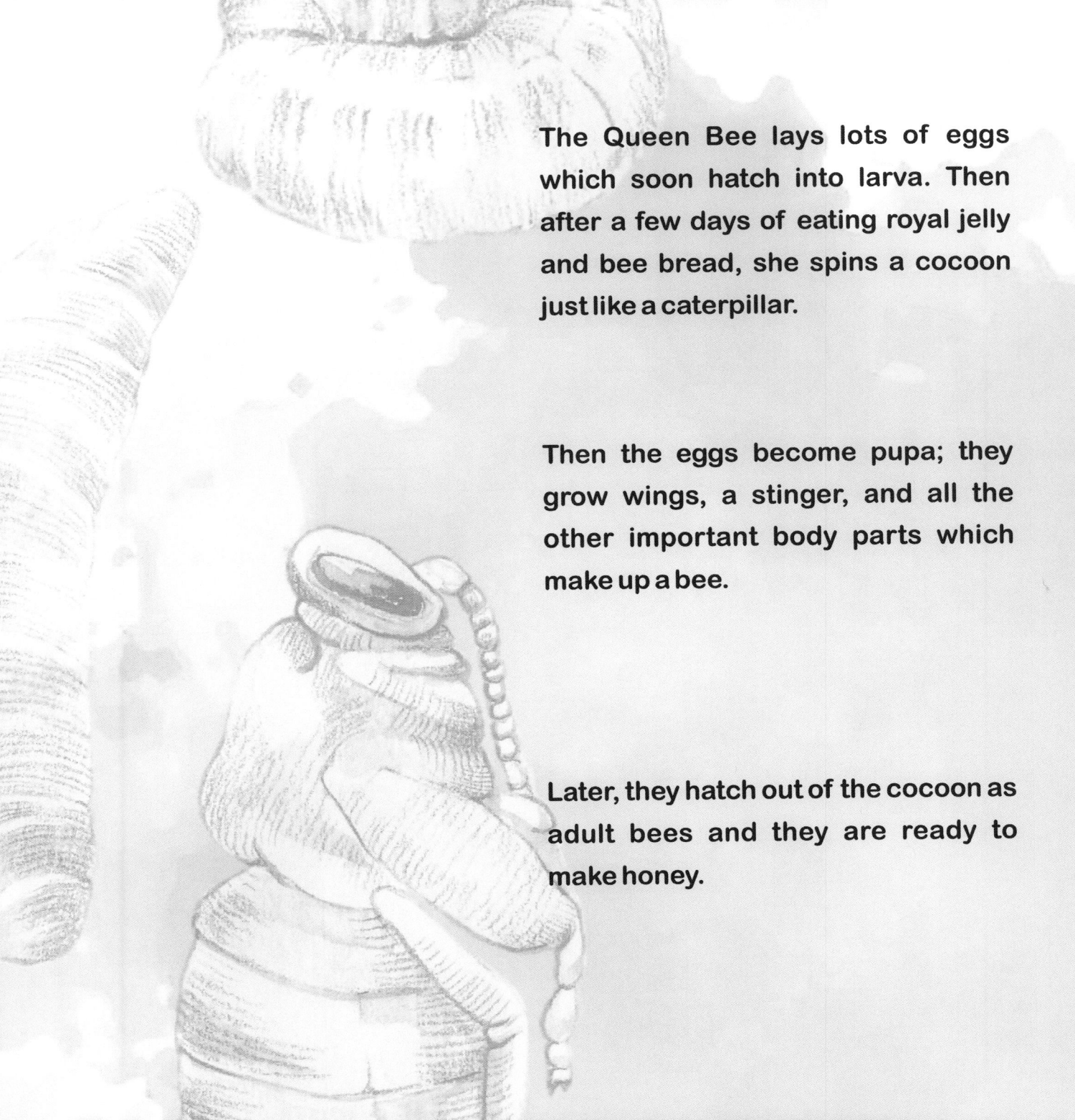

The Queen Bee lays lots of eggs which soon hatch into larva. Then after a few days of eating royal jelly and bee bread, she spins a cocoon just like a caterpillar.

Then the eggs become pupa; they grow wings, a stinger, and all the other important body parts which make up a bee.

Later, they hatch out of the cocoon as adult bees and they are ready to make honey.

Bees not only make honey, but also help to grow fruit and veggies which make you strong and healthy.

We are called pollen gatherers or pollinators. It is not only us; there are lots of other pollinators, such as butterflies, wasps, flies, and hummingbirds.

Who are the pollinators?

As bees fly from flower to flower, pollen sticks to their fuzz and passes between the flowers. Later it helps plants to grow fruit. That is pollination.

Now you know that bees are very important. If we were not here, you would not survive, because you need us to pollinate the plants which give you fruit and vegetables to eat.

Some plants are only pollinated by bees, which means that if we become extinct then they will too.

Farming

Bees are in big trouble because we are losing our habitats. People are taking our space for farming and urban areas.

Loss of Habitat
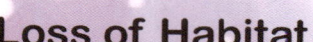

Climate change means that the temperature is becoming too hot so that we cannot live in our habitats. Winter is becoming too hot, so we wake up earlier from hibernation than we usually do. However, the flowers have still not grown, so there is no food ready for us.

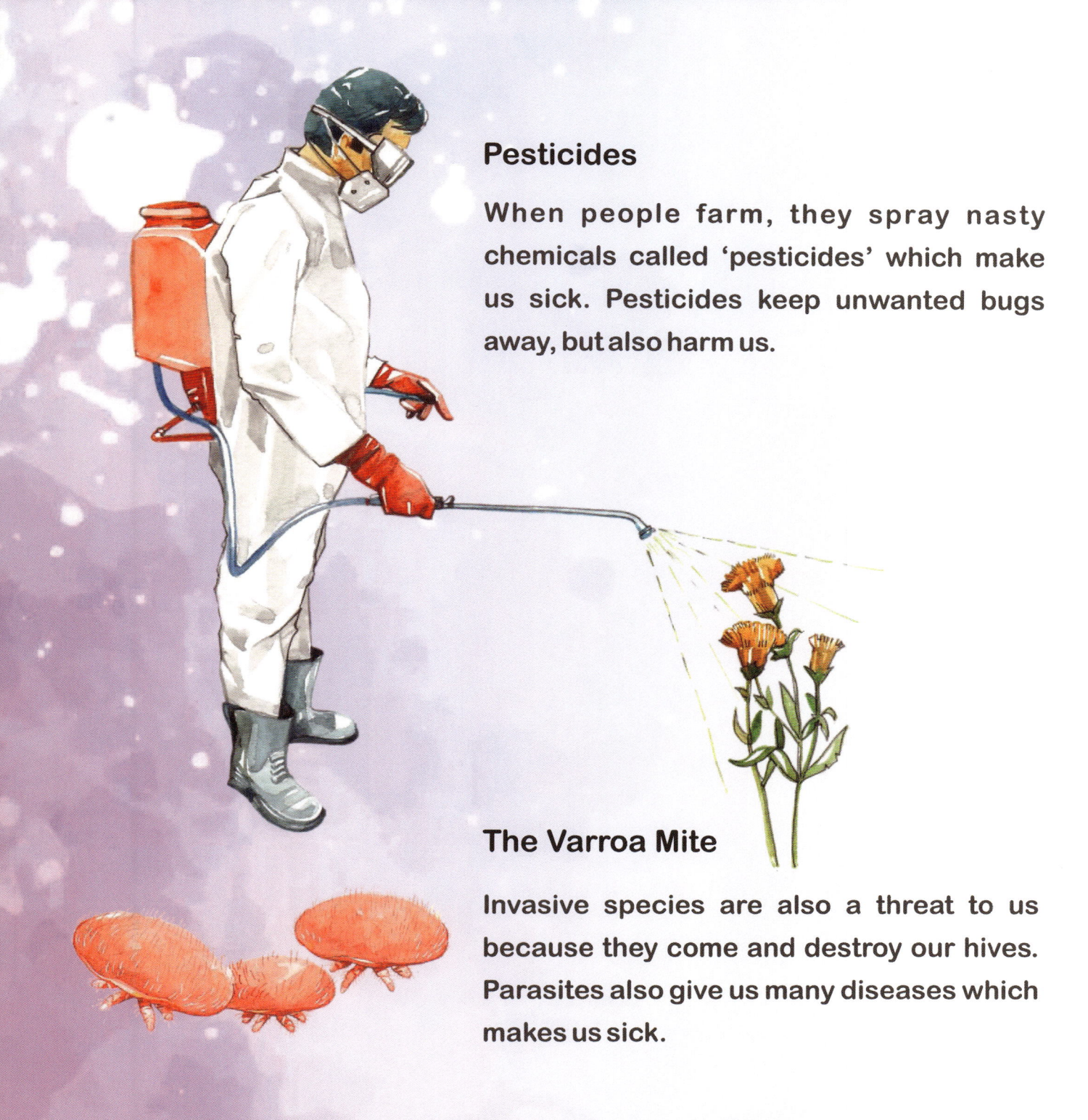

Pesticides

When people farm, they spray nasty chemicals called 'pesticides' which make us sick. Pesticides keep unwanted bugs away, but also harm us.

The Varroa Mite

Invasive species are also a threat to us because they come and destroy our hives. Parasites also give us many diseases which makes us sick.

Let me tell you how to be bee friendly.

1. Grow bee friendly plants

You do not need a big garden for this, you can just use a few pots. Bees love traditional cottage garden flowers and native wild flowers, like primroses, buddleia and marigolds in a variety of different colours. Grow different plants for different seasons so that bees can gather nectar throughout the year.

2. Bee a lazy gardener

Leave your garden a bit messy so the bees have an opportunity to forage. Don't be afraid to leave your garden alone; the good thing is you don't need to worry about your garden for a while. It's a win-win!

3. Bee Kind!

Don't spray. Please do not spray your garden with pesticides and herbicides because they can hurt the pollinators, especially bees.

Those chemicals do get rid of unnecessary bugs, but they hurt useful bugs like us too.

4. Help to protect our habitat

Don't worry if you live in a big city. You can still help the bees by supporting groups and organisations who are working hard to save us.

Tell your parents to vote for a political party which cares about our planet.

5. Learn about pollinators

Kids, you have a big job to do, because you are the future. You need to learn about bees, so tell your friends about bees and most importantly bee friendly!

6. Become a beekeeper

It is fun to be a beekeeper. In this way you can protect the bees and protect the planet too.

HOW TO MAKE A BEE HOTEL

Here's how to make your own bee hotel from a few basic supplies. Remember ask an adult for help when using sharp objects.

To make your bee hotel, you will need:
- An empty, clean tin can
- Bamboo canes
- Secateurs
- String

Cut your bamboo canes so that they fit in the tin can. An easy way to do this is to stand the cane in the tin can and cut it where it reaches the top.

Fill the tin can with canes. Fit as many in as possible, until it's nice and full. Lie the tin can on its side and tie two lengths of string around it, one at each end. Tie the four loose lengths of string together at the ends to create a hanging loop.

Hang your bee hotel in the garden. Somewhere in full sun or partial shade is ideal.

Glossary

Backbone - The line of bones down the centre of the back that provides support for the body.

Compound eye - They are the big, noticeable eyes at the side of the insect's head and allows insects to see in multiple directions and a wider scope than human eyes.

Thorax - The area of the body between the neck and the stomach.

Solitary - Lives alone or without companions.

Hexagon – Shape with six straight sides and angles.

Extinct – completely wiped out or dead.

Habitat – A place where in which an animal or plant usually lives.

Urban areas - towns, cities where many people live

Hibernation - the condition or period of an animal or plant spending the winter in an inactive state.

Parasites - creature survives in or on another species

Enzymes - Makes things easier to digest